new jewish tunes.

ruach 5769
songbook

includes CD (also available separately)

Editors
Michael Boxer
Jayson Rodovsky

Typesetter
Joshua Wiczer

TRANSCONTINENTAL
MUSIC Publications
The world's leading publisher of Jewish music since 1938

Visit **www.RuachCD.com**

for artist information, educational material, and downloads

RUACH 5769 SONGBOOK: NEW JEWISH TUNES

© 2009 Transcontinental Music Publications
CD © 2008 Transcontinental Music Publications
A division of URJ Books and Music
633 Third Avenue - New York, NY 10017 - Fax 212.650.4119
212.650.4105 - **www.TranscontinentalMusic.com** - tmp@urj.org
993358

Manufactured in the United States of America
Cover design by Pine Point Productions - Windham, ME
Book design by Joel N. Eglash
Additional design by Michael Boxer
ISBN 8074-1128-5
10 9 8 7 6 5 4 3 2 1

PREFACE

RUACH IS THE HEBREW WORD FOR *SPIRIT*. It is exactly *that* quality which the songs of the *Ruach* series possess. These songs were chosen for their ear-catching melodies, their colorful instrumental support, and for the life the music breathes into their texts. In short, all this is summed up by one common trait: *ruach*.

The *Ruach* series is the continuation of the seven original NFTY (North American Federation of Temple Youth) albums that were recorded between 1972 and 1989 (see the NFTY five-CD set available from Transcontinental Music). The NFTY and *Ruach* albums are primary sources of participatory music for cantors, songleaders, musical leaders and all those who disseminate Jewish music. Through their leadership, the tradition of singing is passed on to the next generation of campers and youth groupers: the future songleaders, cantors, and musical leaders. This songbook is another way of preserving this musical tradition for future generations.

Joel N. Eglash
Series Creator

Thanks are due to Loui Dobin, Steve Fontaine, Rabbi Dan Freelander, Jonathan Levine,
Rabbi Michael Mellen, Victor Ney, Rachel Wetstein; the members of the *Ruach 5769* committee,
whose varying backgrounds and experiences helped shape this remarkable collection of music;
and, of course, the artists who have created this great music for all of us.

RUACH 5769 COMMITTEE

Michael Boxer
Steve Brodsky
Adrian Durlester
Joel N. Eglash
Michael Goldberg
Jessica Goodman
Cantor Alane Katzew
Eric Komar
Caryn Roman
Rebecca Rosenfeld
Carine Warsawski

Hebrew Pronunciation Guide

VOWELS
a as in *father*
ai as in *aisle* (= long *i* as in *ice*)
e = short *e* as in *bed*
ei as in *eight* (= long *a* as in *ace*)
i as in *pizza* (= long *e* as in *be*)
o = long *o* as in *go*
u = long *u* as in *lunar*
' = unstressed vowel close to ə or unstressed short *e*

CONSONANTS
ch as in German *Bach* or Scottish *loch* (not as in *cheese*)
g = hard *g* as in **get** (not soft *g* as in **gem**)
tz = as in *boats*
h after a vowel is silent

ruach 5769

ruach 5769 songbook

someday *by* michelle citrin

text & music: michelle citrin

So often we look around and talk about how different we would like things to be. And so often, we don't do anything about it. *Someday* was inspired by the very wise words of Rabbi Hillel, "Im lo achshav, eimatai" (If not now, then when?), a phrase that I wear proudly on a ring, always reminding me to remember the importance of living in the moment.

4

or chadash by dan nichols and e18hteen

new light

hebrew: liturgy
music & english: dan nichols

The Hebrew is an excerpt from a prayer in the Jewish morning liturgy, *Yotzeir Or*. It's interesting that the Reform Movement removed this Hebrew phrase from *Gates of Prayer*, and only recently returned the phrase to the new Reform Movement prayer book, *Mishkan T'filah*. Rabbi Jan Katzew commissioned me to write this for his wife, Cantor Alane Katzew, in honor of her 50th birthday. My inspiration came from a trip to Israel. I was surprised by the tension that I felt, heard, and witnessed everywhere. The Hebrew can be translated as: "Shine a new light upon Zion, that we all may swiftly merit its radiance."

Copyright © 2008 Dan Nichols

אוֹר חָדָשׁ עַל צִיּוֹן תָּאִיר,
וְנִזְכֶּה כֻלָּנוּ מְהֵרָה לְאוֹרוֹ.

Shine a new light upon Zion,
that we all may swiftly merit its radiance.

tree of life by todd herzog

eitz chayim hi

text & music: todd herzog

> I was not raised with a strong Jewish background. Over the past five years, I have become much more involved with Judaism, but I needed to find a way to relate the wisdom contained in the religion to my own life. Music has always been my doorway to deeper understanding. This song is my own semi-autobiographical version of how the process of transferring our knowledge, from generation to generation, actually works.

Instrumental Introduction

With Energy (♩ = 92)

1. It was plan-ted by my grand-pa in his wis-dom and his fore-thought to pro-vide shade and pro-tec-tion for our fam - i - ly. As he fin-ished with his toil he looked up at me from the soil and I ne-ver will for-get the words he said to me: If you hold on tight to this tree of life you will lead a life of jus-tice and in-te-gri-ty. If you